BROOKLANDS COLLEGE LIBRARY
~~ ~~^^ WEYBRIDGE, SURREY KT1 2X~

Telephone Skills that Satisfy Customers

Unleash the full potential of the telephone

Rick Conlow
Doug Watsabaugh

A Crisp Fifty-Minute™ Series Book

BROOKLANDS COLLEGE LIBRARY

106787

Telephone Skills that Satisfy Customers
Unleash the full potential of the telephone

Rick Conlow
Doug Watsabaugh

CREDITS:

President, Axzo Press:	**Jon Winder**
Vice President, Product Development:	**Charles G. Blum**
Vice President, Operations:	**Josh Pincus**
Director, Publishing Systems Development:	**Dan Quackenbush**

COPYRIGHT © 2009 Axzo Press. All Rights Reserved.

No part of this work may be reproduced, transcribed, or used in any form or by any means—graphic, electronic, or mechanical, including photocopying, recording, taping, Web distribution, or information storage and retrieval systems—without the prior written permission of the publisher.

For more information, go to **www.CrispSeries.com**

Trademarks

Crisp Fifty-Minute Series is a trademark of Axzo Press.

Some of the product names and company names used in this book have been used for identification purposes only and may be trademarks or registered trademarks of their respective manufacturers and sellers.

Disclaimer

We reserve the right to revise this publication and make changes from time to time in its content without notice.

ISBN 10: 1-4260-1846-0
ISBN 13: 978-1-4260-1846-6

Printed in the United States of America

1 2 3 4 5 6 7 8 9　11 10 09

Table of Contents

About the Authors 1

Preface 3

About the Crisp 50-Minute Series 9

A Note to Instructors 10

Part 1: Keeping a Positive Attitude   11

Why Keeping a Positive Attitude Is Important 13

My Successes and Achievements 17

I Like Myself! 19

Positive Self-Direction 22

Part Summary 28

Part 2: Answering the Telephone Brilliantly   29

Preparing to Answer the Telephone 31

Phone Answering Skills 35

Part Summary 44

Part 3: Asking Questions and Listening Effectively   45

What Customers Want When they Call 47

Ask Questions 50

Listen 53

Take Action 59

Part Summary 62

Part 4: Handling Customer Moments of Truth   63

Customer Focus 65

Moments of Truth 67

Part Summary 78

Part 5: Adding Value   79

Five Strategies for Adding Value 81

Communicate Positively with Others 82

Show the Customer Appreciation 84

Follow Up and Follow Through 89

Go the Extra Mile 90

Create Internal Teamwork 93

Part Summary 98

Appendix 99

Appendix to Part 2 101

Appendix to Part 3 103

Appendix to Part 4 104

Appendix to Part 5 105

Additional Reading 108

About the Authors

Rick Conlow

A quick glance at his professional résumé leaves you with the strong impression that effort and optimism are a winning combination. Case in point: With Rick by their side, clients have achieved double- and triple-digit improvement in their sales performance, quality, customer loyalty, and service results over the past 20-plus years and earned more than 30 quality and service awards.

In an age where optimism and going the extra mile can sound trite, Rick has made them a differentiator. His clients include organizations that lead their industries, as well as others that are less recognizable. Regardless, their goals are his goals.

Rick's life view and extensive background in sales and leadership—as a general manager, vice president, training director, program director, national sales trainer, and consultant—are the foundation of his coaching, training, and consulting services. Participants in Rick's experiential "live action" programs walk away with ah-ha's, inspiration, and skills they can immediately put to use. These programs include "BEST Selling!"; "Moments of Magic!"; "Excellence in Management!"; "SuperSTAR Service and Selling!"; "The Greatest Secrets of all Time!"; and "Good Boss/Bad Boss—Which One Are You?" Rick has also written *Excellence in Management*, *Excellence in Supervision*, *Returning to Learning*, and *Moments of Magic*.

When he's not engaging an audience or engrossed in a coaching discussion, this proud husband and father is most likely astride a weight bench or riding a motorcycle, taking on the back roads and highways of Minnesota.

Doug Watsabaugh

Doug values being a "regular person," with his feet on the ground and his head in the realities of the daily challenges his clients face. It's his caring about and experience in helping clients deal with difficult situations that distinguish him from other sales performance and leadership development consultants.

His knowledge of experiential learning and his skill in designing change processes and learning events have enabled him to measurably improve the lives of thousands of individuals and hundreds of organizations in a wide variety of industries— financial services, manufacturing, medical devices, consumer goods, and technology, to name a few.

Before starting his own business, Doug served as the director of operations for a national training institute, was the manager of organizational development for a major chemical company, and was responsible for worldwide training and organization development for the world's third largest toy company.

He was also a partner in Performance & Human Development LLC, a California company that published high-involvement experiential activities, surveys and instruments, interactive training modules, papers, and multimedia presentations.

Doug has co-written two books with John E. Jones, Ph.D., and William L. Bearley, Ed. D.: *The New Fieldbook for Trainers,* published by HRD Press and Lakewood Publishing, and *The OUS Quality Item Pool*, about organizational survey items that measure Baldrige criteria. Doug is a member of the American Society for Training and Development (ASTD), the Minnesota Quality Council, and The National Organization Development Network.

Doug's father taught him the value of hard work, and it paid dividends: He funded his college education by playing guitar and singing with a rock-and-roll band, experiencing a close call with fame when he played bass in concert with Chuck Berry. Not bad for a guy who admits to being "a bit shy." While Doug's guitar remains a source of enjoyment, it pales in comparison to his "number one joy and priority," his family.

WCW Partners

WCW Partners is a performance improvement company with more than 20 years of experience helping companies, governmental agencies, and nonprofit organizations worldwide revitalize their results and achieve record-breaking performance. We are experts in sales performance, organizational development, leadership development, marketing, and communications—and we don't mind telling you that we're different from most consulting firms you'll find in the marketplace.

For one thing, it's our approach; when you hire us, you get us. But just as important, we're people who've had to wrestle with the same issues you have—how to strengthen sales, boost productivity, improve quality, increase employee satisfaction, build a team, or retain and attract new customers. To us, "We develop the capability in you" is more than a catchy phrase. It's our promise.

Our clients include 3M, American Express, American Medical Systems, Amgen Inc., Accenture, AmeriPride Services, Andersen Windows, Avanade, Beltone, Canadian Linen and Uniform Service, Carew International, Case Corporation, Citigroup, Coca-Cola, Costco, Covance, Deknatel, Eaton Corporation, Electrochemicals Inc., Entergy, Esoterix, General Mills, GN Resound, Grant Thornton, Hasbro Inc., Honeywell, Interton, Kenner Products, Marketlink, Kemps-Marigold, Meijer Corporation, National Computer Systems, Parker Brothers, Toro, Productive Workplace Systems, Red Wing Shoes, Rite Aid, Rollerblade, Ryan Companies, Travelers Insurance, Thrivent, Tonka Corporation, and a number of nonprofit and educational institutions.

To learn how you can do amazing things, visit us online at WCWPartners.com, or contact Doug or Rick toll-free at 1-888-313-0514.

Preface

Nearly all of us use the phone in our jobs. Superstar customer service demands superstar telephone skills. Too many people and organizations take the phone for granted. After all, it's been around since March 7, 1876, invented and patented by Alexander Graham Bell.

Imagine that you are the customer in these situations:

1. You call a retail store to check on a potential order. The phone rings and rings. No one answers.

2. You call a car dealership to see if it has a part for your car. You get the parts department. The person answers with a curt "Hello." You tell the person what you need, and he clunks the phone on the counter and says, "Harry, do we have…." He comes back and says, "Can't help ya."

3. You call a credit card company to question a charge on your bill. You are transferred four times and then get cut off.

4. You call your health insurer to check on payment of a bill. The finance department clerk answers the phone and says quickly, "Can you hold?" She puts you on hold abruptly, and you wait, listening to awful music. After a couple of minutes, she comes back and says, "Can you give me your policy number?"

5. You call the local home improvement store to add to an existing order that is to be delivered. The customer service person answers the phone with a friendly greeting. As you give him your information, he interrupts and says, "There is no order. You will have to come in to get this taken care of." Then he hangs up.

How would you feel in these situations? How you would react to this kind of telephone customer service is also how your customers would probably react. In each situation, the company is in danger of losing a customer because of the poor phone etiquette and overall customer service.

Companies spend millions of dollars to attract customers through advertisements on TV, on the radio, on the Web, and through direct mail. Unfortunately, it takes only a matter of seconds to derail that effort and send a customer elsewhere.

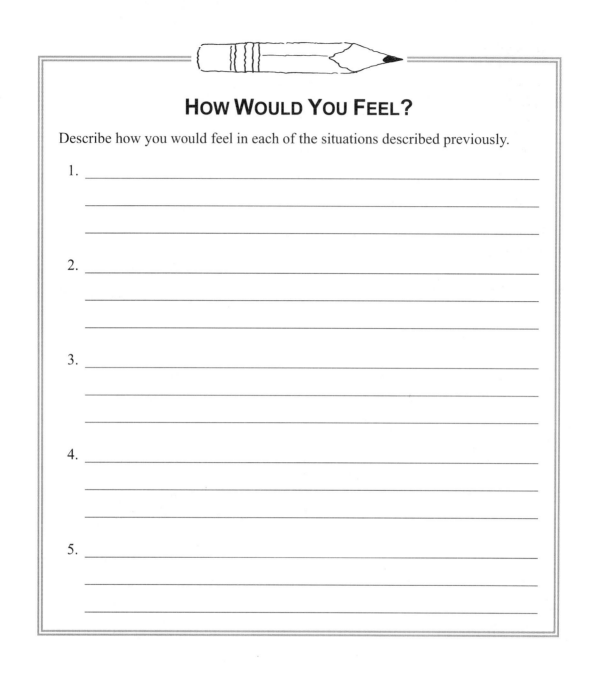

HOW WOULD YOU FEEL?

Describe how you would feel in each of the situations described previously.

1. _____

   _____

   _____

2. _____

   _____

   _____

3. _____

   _____

   _____

4. _____

   _____

   _____

5. _____

   _____

   _____

SuperSTAR Customer Service: A Definition

Our other book, *SuperSTAR Customer Service*, provides the framework for exemplary service. It defines three levels of moments of truth. These apply to dealing with customers over the telephone as well:

▶ **Moment of misery** — When you do less than the customer expects.

▶ **Moment of mediocrity** — When you only meet a customer's expectation.

▶ **Moment of magic** — When you exceed the customer's expectation.

A *moment of truth* is anything you do that directly affects the customer's perception of you or your organization.

SuperSTAR Customer Service

Treating customers much better than they expect by self-managing moments of magic.

SuperSTAR Telephone Skills More Than Satisfy Customers

E-mail and instant messaging are becoming critical ways to communicate today, yet the importance of the phone is even greater. With the advent of cell phone use, fewer calls are screened through a professional receptionist, so effective telephone etiquette has deteriorated rapidly. It's your opportunity and responsibility to handle phone calls professionally. The content of this book applies to the desk or office phone and the cell phone.

We will focus on areas for using the telephone properly and professionally, and work on turning them into moments of magic for your customers so they keep coming back. These areas are:

▶ Keeping a positive attitude

▶ Answering the telephone brilliantly

▶ Asking questions and listening effectively

▶ Handling customer moments of truth

▶ Giving added value

" *Customer service is the best business strategy of all.***"**

–Anonymous

Too many of us dispense with effective phone skills because of all the distractions we face. Although this tends to happen, these aren't appropriate excuses.

TOP 10 DISTRACTIONS

Check (✓) the distractions you regularly face:

- ❑ Other projects on your computer
- ❑ The Internet
- ❑ Drop-in visitors
- ❑ Other phone calls
- ❑ E-mail messages arriving on your computer

- ❑ Noise from other people
- ❑ Meetings that are going on or that you have to go to
- ❑ Mail
- ❑ Personal calls or issues
- ❑ Yourself—tired, bored, lazy, or indifferent

- ❑ Other: _____
- ❑ Other: _____

The Bottom Line

Research from a variety of sources, such as the Technical Assistance Research Project, the U.S. Office of Consumer Affairs, and the Product Marketing and Profit Impact Marketing Strategy, shows that companies with the best service:

▶ Charge more for their products

▶ Enjoy stronger customer retention

▶ Gain market share

▶ Make more profit

▶ Offer greater job security and more opportunities to their employees

Most companies and industries use some form of customer survey to get feedback from customers on the quality of their service. (Find out how your company does this, and keep abreast of the results.) Organizations like J.D. Power and Associates, the Consumers Union (publisher of *Consumer Reports*), and the University of Michigan (which conducts the Customer Satisfaction Index survey) also rate companies across industries. Why? For the reasons mentioned above. You can categorize service in three ways:

▶ Poor

▶ Average

▶ Excellent

Poor Service

"Poor service" means a lack of concern or care. Unfortunately, some people might be better suited for jobs in the back room or might benefit from extensive training. This group includes the waitress who walked up to a couple in her section, stuck out a hip, and said, "Hurry up and order. I'm on break in a few minutes!" This group includes traders who sold worthless derivatives to their clients. Did these people want to satisfy their customers?

Average Service

"Average" service is only mediocre. There was once a retailer that had been #1 for years. If people needed clothes, tools, appliances, or electronics, they patronized this company. However, the company became so large that it lost focus and seemed to lose sight of customers' changing needs.

Being average means that you don't get better, and if there are problems, you point your finger in another direction. Average customer service reps do just enough to get by. Yet, companies in this category can't say they are average. Could you imagine a company with the slogan, "We are no worse than anyone else"? Wow! Now that's a phrase to motivate employees and customers alike. Instead, these companies claim to provide good service. In reality, they do little to distinguish themselves.

Excellent Service

"Excellent" customer service people really care, have great attitudes, and extend themselves to make customers feel special. The people or companies who fall into this category are better, faster, and different. These attributes help employees get promoted and rise to the top in their companies. The best companies in any industry tend to have the best customer service.

Excellent service is the waitress who smiles, pays attention to you, and has a sense of humor. It's the airline attendant who greets you when you get on the plane and creates a fun atmosphere for the trip. It's the friendly employees in a grocery store who go out of their way to help you. It's the plumber who explains what he did and calls back later to see if everything is still okay. And it's the pharmacist who is courteous and helpful and takes time for your questions. Excellent performers routinely go the extra mile and add value. These people become the superstars, both in person and on the telephone.

Learning Objectives

Complete this book, and you'll know how to:

1) Keep a positive attitude, and understand how setting goals can help with that.

2) Prepare yourself to deal with people on the phone, and answer the phone effectively and professionally.

3) Ask questions, listen effectively, and take action to meet customers' needs.

4) Assess your own customer focus, and handle the seven moments of truth for customer service on the telephone.

5) Add value to set yourself and your company apart so that customers want to work with you.

Workplace and Management Competencies mapping

For over 30 years, business and industry has utilized competency models to select employees. The trend to use competency-based approaches in education and training, assessment, and development of workers has experienced a more recent emergence within the Employment and Training Administration (ETA), a division of the United States Department of Labor.

The ETA's General Competency Model Framework spans a wide array of competencies from the more basic competencies, such as reading and writing, to more advanced occupation-specific competencies. The Crisp Series finds its home in what the ETA refers to as the Workplace Competencies and the Management Competencies.

Telephone Skills that Satisfy Customers covers information vital to mastering the following competencies:

Workplace Competencies:

▶ Customer Focus

▶ Problem Solving & Decision Making

For a comprehensive mapping of Crisp Series titles to the Workplace and Management competencies, visit www.CrispSeries.com.

About the Crisp 50-Minute Series

The Crisp 50-Minute Series was designed to cover critical business and professional development topics in the shortest possible time. Our easy-to-read, easy-to-understand format can be used for self-study or for classroom training. With a wealth of hands-on exercises, the 50-Minute books keep you engaged and help you retain critical skills.

What You Need to Know

We designed the Crisp 50-Minute Series to be as self-explanatory as possible. But there are a few things you should know before you begin the book.

Exercises

Exercises look like this:

EXERCISE TITLE

Questions and other information would be here.

Keep a pencil handy. Any time you see an exercise, you should try to complete it. If the exercise has specific answers, an answer key will be provided in the appendix. (Some exercises ask you to think about your own opinions or situation; these types of exercises will not have answer keys.)

Forms

A heading like this means that the rest of the page is a form:

FORMHEAD

Forms are meant to be reusable. You might want to make a photocopy of a form before you fill it out, so that you can use it again later.

A Note to Instructors

We've tried to make the Crisp 50-Minute Series books as useful as possible as classroom training manuals. Here are some of the features we provide for instructors:

▶ PowerPoint presentations

▶ Answer keys

▶ Assessments

▶ Customization

PowerPoint Presentations

You can download a PowerPoint presentation for this book from our Web site at www.CrispSeries.com.

Answer keys

If an exercise has specific answers, an answer key will be provided in the appendix. (Some exercises ask you to think about your own opinions or situation; these types of exercises will not have answer keys.)

Assessments

For each 50-Minute Series book, we have developed a 35- to 50-item assessment. The assessment for this book is available at www.CrispSeries.com. *Assessments should not be used in any employee-selection process.*

Customization

Crisp books can be quickly and easily customized to meet your needs—from adding your logo to developing proprietary content. Crisp books are available in print and electronic form. For more information on customization, see www.CrispSeries.com.

Keeping a
Positive Attitude

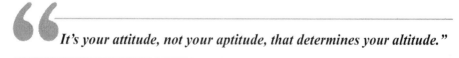

It's your attitude, not your aptitude, that determines your altitude."

–Zig Ziglar

In this part:

- ▶ How a positive attitude affects customer satisfaction and retention
- ▶ How your successes and achievements feed your positive attitude
- ▶ How goal-setting can give you positive self-direction

Why Keeping a Positive Attitude Is Important

Why provide excellent customer service on the phone? Quite simply, the success or failure of your business is determined by your success in meeting customer needs. Many businesses prosper or fail based on word of mouth alone. Word travels fast if you are the best at meeting customer needs, and it travels even faster if your service is bad.

Companies like Disney, Southwest Airlines, and Nordstrom's have become famous for having great service. Joe Girard, world-famous car salesman, says, "Let me sell you a lemon so I can show you how good my service department is."

There is no faster way to develop loyal long-term customers than to be there when a problem develops and resolve it to the customer's satisfaction. Likewise, there is no faster way to drive customers away than to put them off or try to blame a problem on them or others. Customer service can cost you in the short term, but pays tremendous dividends in the long term.

People in customer service roles include anyone in the company who serves the customer or serves someone who does. The receptionist, manager, customer service rep, CEO, sales rep, or computer technician can make or break customer service one customer at a time. *The telephone is on the front line of this, and the way it's used produces the first and most important impression of a company.*

Some research estimates that the attitude of employees accounts for 80% of a company's customer service image and whether or not a customer comes back. That's an enormous responsibility.

OBSTACLES TO EXCELLENT SERVICE

Keeping a positive attitude can be hard sometimes. Customers can be demanding, unreasonable, and rude. Other obstacles, like technology failures or confusing company policies, can make it tough to provide extraordinary service.

List three or four experiences you have had that make it difficult to do an excellent job.

1. _____

_____

2. _____

_____

3. _____

_____

4. _____

_____

Positive Self-Awareness

You may be wondering how this relates to the telephone. Dealing with obstacles and keeping a positive attitude begins and ends with you. Your greatest gift is the ability to choose your own thinking and therefore your actions. The first step in taking care of the customer on the phone has nothing to do with the customer; it has everything thing to do with you and your attitude.

If you are upset and choose to stew about a situation, your mood can spill over onto the next customer you talk to. If you are irritated by a new company policy, your irritation can leak out on the next phone contact. We know a telemarketing company that has this philosophy: "Smile before you dial." They put mirrors in front of their reps because if they smile genuinely as they call customers, they make 15% more sales. So you need to have a method to stay positive no matter what. Neither you nor your company can afford to let poor attitudes cause a customer to get angry or to defect.

Let's review two main strategies to help you stay positive when things are going well and when they aren't going so well. The first one is self-awareness.

In our *SuperSTAR Customer Service* book, we use this quote from *Hamlet*: "To thine own self be true." This is the first step in providing excellent service. Let's add to that here.

Positive self-awareness is about conducting a personal review, looking at your strengths and areas to improve in, and being honest in the process. After all, your view of yourself is the foundation of all that you think and all of your actions, including providing customer service on the phone.

A Launching Pad to SuperSTAR Telephone Skills

Before you can reach a destination, you have to have a starting point. The space shuttle has a launching pad; a plane ticket lists the city of departure; every book has a table of contents; and every building has a foundation.

Effective customer service and good telephone skills require the same thing. Too often, motivational speakers or teachers emphasize big dreams and goals. Those are important, but you need to understand where you are starting from before you can decide where you want to go and take the actions required to provide service excellence.

> **The first step to success is self esteem."**
>
> **–Ralph Waldo Emerson**

"Computer servers we got, customer servers we no got."

LAUNCHING PAD

This exercise begins the process of identifying your support structure for positive thinking. It identifies that inner spirit and drive to do well. If you don't recognize your talents, you limit yourself and what you can achieve in your job. The future is the only part of your life you can control and create, and the future begins today. Understand and accept this, and you will begin to move forward from your present results to consistently delivering moments of magic.

What really motivates me is:	What I like about my job is:
People can count on me because:	**My customers think of me as:**
To me, success means:	**I am a superstar because:**

My Successes and Achievements

Have you ever noticed how a bright, sunny day often lifts the spirits of people? They seem happier, more in tune with and excited about life. This is especially true if the weather has been rainy, cloudy, or snowy for a while.

Peoples' feelings about themselves seem to change often, depending on their life circumstances. People tend to keep mental scorecards to record when they are ahead or behind in life. Too often, they see themselves on the losing end. For example, one psychological study indicated that people have over 50,000 thoughts a day, and over 85% of those thoughts are negative. Is there any wonder that the world is full of problems, disorders, and strife? What we think (over extended periods of time), we become. Negative thoughts get negative results; positive thoughts get positive results. Throughout history, philosophers and teachers have expressed this premise time and again.

So how do we change our results to make them more positive? Positive thinking begins by creating positive images about other people, the world, and ourselves. It sounds simple, but it works. In other words, as trainer and motivator John O'Dell says, "How you see yourself today determines your tomorrow."

Why not give yourself a pat on the back for a change? This has nothing to do with bragging or getting a big head, but rather is about just recognizing the way things are. Too often, people are quick to shrug off a compliment or a victory. Instead, they concentrate on the negative.

You are an achiever by nature. Make a list of your successes, achievements, or things you have done that you are proud of, and add to it often. Why? Because it is your core and what makes up who you are. It's what will drive you forward to serve customers well on the phone, even when it is hard to do. Use this list to remind yourself about your abilities and what you can accomplish.

> *"There is no self-improvement, only increasing in the ability to be all that you already are."*
>
> **–Anonymous**

My Successes and Achievements

This exercise is designed to help you remember your successes and achievements and to help you see yourself in a positive way. Some people say, "I haven't had many successes." The truth is, you have! You may have made mistakes or had a failure or two. You have also achieved many things. First, accept the possibility that this is true. Then, identify your successes or achievements. Fill in the circle completely.

Here are a couple of examples: attending school, helping others in need, being a good friend, or winning an award in school or at work. To achieve service excellence consistently, you need to think this way about life and yourself!

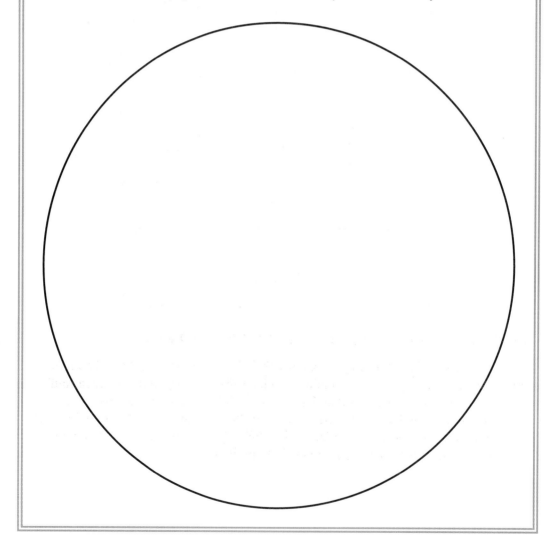

I Like Myself!

You really are a special and important person! According to medical research, the odds of your DNA looking similar to someone else's are 1 in 37 million. And your DNA map will be different in obvious ways. You possess unique positive qualities, experiences, knowledge, thoughts, attitudes, and insights that make you a success today. You have good reason to feel good about yourself. You can be a superstar customer service provider on the phone or in person!

A basic drive of human beings is to feel good about their lives. This need fuels a person's inner motivations and self-esteem. Begin serving your customers on the phone with a fresh perspective. At first glance, how many squares do you see below?

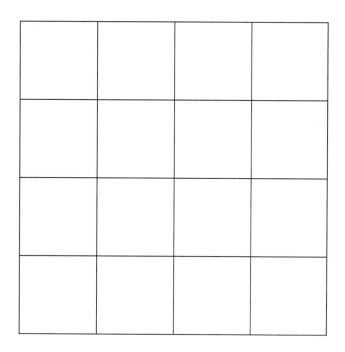

People most often say 16 or 17. Look closer—there are 30 squares.

Look at yourself the same way. Expand your personal perception. First, be more positive! Then, seek your hidden talents and abilities. Bobby Kennedy once said, "Some people look at the world and ask why? I look at the world and ask, why not?" Scientists say that people use only 1% of their potential in a lifetime. To be a superstar customer service provider on the phone, you have to work at it and be persistent. You have to believe in it and want to do it.

I LIKE MYSELF!

Lift yourself above any weaknesses, failures, or adversities you have faced. Be aware of them, work to overcome them, but don't use them as an excuse to hold yourself down in life. Firmly believe that you are increasing your ability to be all that you really are. Work on building your self-confidence and confirming your unlimited potential. Do it now! Take the next few minutes to pat yourself on the back, to like yourself. Answer the questions below.

1. List one important, positive decision or event that helped direct your life:

   _____

   _____

2. List two of the most important values that motivate and excite you about life, and describe why. (For example, "honesty—integrity is important to a good life.")

   _____

   _____

3. List three areas of your life that you want to continue to grow in and develop:

   _____

   _____

   _____

CONTINUED

4. Identify four people who have had a positive influence on your life. What positive quality do you remember about each person?

_____

_____

_____

_____

5. Write five positive qualities that you possess (for example: good listener):

_____

_____

_____

_____

_____

6. Complete this phrase: I like myself because…

_____

_____

Positive Self-Direction

What is success, after all? Money, bank accounts, stock market success, Internet fame, or a Ph.D.? An article in the *Washington Post* a few years back gave some clues. It described two people. The first was a lobbyist who made a six-figure income. He lived in the most expensive neighborhood and interacted with the highest government officials. He said his life had no meaning. The other person was a single parent who finished high school by taking night classes. She also worked, making $15,000 a year. She was excited and declared that life was full of possibilities.

Having a positive self-direction is part art and part science. It's an art because it's about determining and creating what you want in life. It's a science because there is a step-by-step process you can follow to do that. With positive self-direction, you can more readily achieve the success you desire. Included in that is your job taking care of customers in person and on the phone.

We will work through three steps:

1. Identify what you want.

2. Set goals.

3. Take the first steps.

Identify What You Want

Ask 100 people what they want, and 95 will tell you what they don't want. They don't want their old cars, debts, aches and pains, or relationships. People have learned that if they ask for what they want, they might not get it. And who needs rejection or failure? Yet without risk, without declaring what you want, life becomes a hit-or-miss affair, often in turmoil.

Begin achieving more success in life by dreaming again. Keep the questions open-ended. Take some time now to think about what you want for your family or yourself. Use your imagination and think of what you want to be, what you want to do, or what you want to have. Relax and picture all the places you want to visit, people you want to meet, things you want to do, careers or jobs you want to have, and how you may want to help others.

> *Success is the progressive realization of predetermined worthwhile goals."*
>
> **–Paul J. Meyer**

IDENTIFYING WHAT YOU WANT

Relax a little—let go. Brainstorm! Don't judge anything. Write your dreams in the spaces below, under Personal and Career. Anything is possible for now; you will narrow the ideas later. Why not really dream again, just as you did as a child? Why not dream the impossible dream?

List 7–10 things in each area. For example: Personal—Hawaii vacation; Career—a college degree.

Personal	Career

Set Goals

The following story might give you a new perspective on any obstacles you face in setting and achieving goals.

Terry Fox

When he was 17, Terry Fox learned that he had cancer in one of his legs. A few days after his eighteenth birthday, the leg was amputated. The night before the operation, Terry dreamed that he was running across Canada.

Soon Terry was fitted with an artificial limb, and he started running across Canada to raise awareness and raise money for cancer research. He began to run across Canada with a goal in mind to help eliminate cancer. He set a goal to raise $1 million for the Cancer Society. After Terry had run three-fifths of the way, the cancer spread, and Terry soon died. He didn't complete his run, yet he raised $24 million for the Cancer Society, and he positively touched the lives of millions of people through his courage and purpose. To date, the Terry Fox foundation has raised over $100 million. People can achieve incredible things, and so can you!

PRIORITIZING GOALS

Review your dream list in the previous exercise ("Identifying What You Want"). In each column, put a star next to three items that you want the most, can believe in, and are willing to set a goal toward.

A goal needs to be specific, not general. For example, consider the difference between the following two items:

▶ Save more money. (This is unspecific and is not a goal.)

▶ Save $3000 ($250 a month) this year for a down payment on a car. (This is specific, with a timeline and a purpose.)

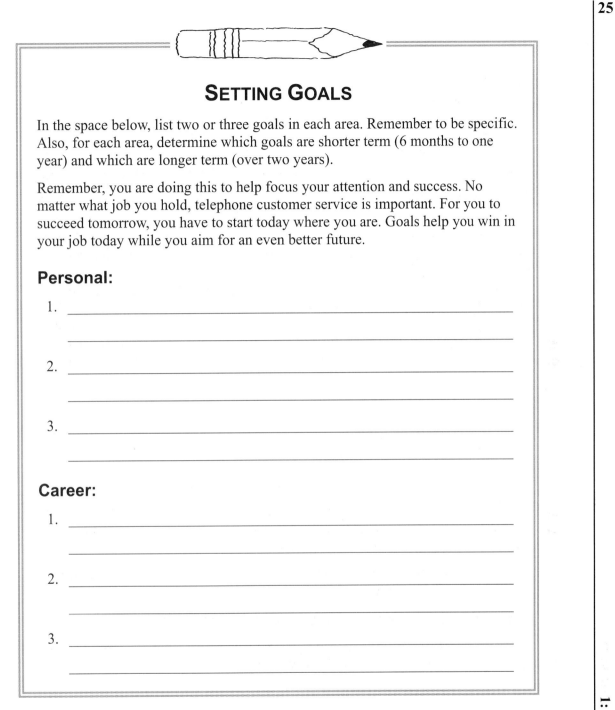

SETTING GOALS

In the space below, list two or three goals in each area. Remember to be specific. Also, for each area, determine which goals are shorter term (6 months to one year) and which are longer term (over two years).

Remember, you are doing this to help focus your attention and success. No matter what job you hold, telephone customer service is important. For you to succeed tomorrow, you have to start today where you are. Goals help you win in your job today while you aim for an even better future.

Personal:

1. _____

   _____

2. _____

   _____

3. _____

   _____

Career:

1. _____

   _____

2. _____

   _____

3. _____

   _____

Take the First Steps

After setting goals at a goal-setting seminar, participants were instructed to take the first step. They were given 10 minutes in the seminar to act on and begin achieving one of their goals. They were then asked what they did and learned. First, they were excited, motivated, and committed. Most made progress. They made phone calls, wrote letters, held meetings, made plans, and spoke to people. They learned to take the first step before taking the next step, and to do a lot in a short time. A tree isn't chopped down with one swing of an axe. It takes many swings, but each one counts. Yes, set goals, but always focus on the first step and take action.

Ask for support. People are social in nature. Contrary to some popular opinions, people need people. When you set a goal, why not share it? Don't share it with everybody. Our world tends to be negative and will criticize you if you scream your goals from a rooftop. But you can share them with a few trusted family members or friends. Ask for their support and help. Ask for their ideas and thoughts to help you take action. Two heads are better than one, aren't they? In addition, share your support with your family and friends. Return their encouragement and positive attitudes.

By sharing their goals, husbands and wives can build commitment and the bond between them. Business partners who share goals can help each other move toward better job performance. Friends who support one another add a deeper meaning and energy to the friendship. There are few people in the world, if any, who wouldn't benefit from the support of a few key, trusted friends.

Then, visualize success. Picture the goals as accomplished. Write them in the present tense and make them positive. "I am a slim 150 pounds" is a better goal than "I am losing 20 pounds." Sports doctors indicate that mental training is just as important as physical training. Olympic trainers require their athletes to create mental images of victory. These images add to the physical training. In a sense, it is a pre-play of the end results.

Finally, *whatever you are doing now, do it well*. In other words, take care of your customer in your current job! Be positive, and make it a goal to be a superstar customer service provider, on the phone and in person.

Read the following customer service facts before you go on to the next part of this book. Note how the last fact relates to keeping a positive attitude.

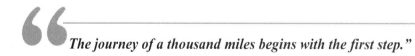

The journey of a thousand miles begins with the first step."

—**A Chinese proverb**

Customer Service Facts

▶ Customer loyalty is estimated to be worth 10 times the price of a single purchase.

▶ Businesses usually spend five to six times more to attract new customers than to retain old ones.

▶ A satisfied customer will tell four to five other people.

▶ An unsatisfied customer will tell eight to ten other people.

▶ An average business has one in four customers with complaints. The average company never hears from 96% of the people with the complaints.

▶ Over 95% of complaints can be handled satisfactorily. These customers tell an average of five other people.

▶ It takes 20 positive moments of truth to overcome one negative one.

▶ If complaints aren't identified, 91% of the unhappy customers will never come back.

▶ The biggest single reason customers have complaints is because of poor or indifferent attitudes from the employees in a company.

BUILDING YOUR POSITIVE ATTITUDE

In the space below, write what you will do to have a positive attitude at work and on the phone.

_____

_____

_____

_____

_____

_____

_____

_____

_____

_____

Part Summary

In this part, we discussed the key points about keeping a positive attitude. You now know that with consistent goal setting, you are the key to your own success. Using what you've learned about yourself, and the methods for staying positive, you will be able to provide excellent customer service and sales by using the telephone.

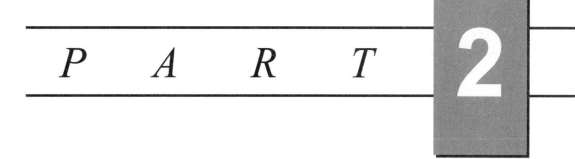

PART 2

Answering the Telephone Brilliantly

Telephone, n. An invention of the devil which abrogates some of the advantages of making a disagreeable person keep his distance.

—Ambrose Bierce

In this part:

▶ How to prepare yourself to answer the phone, and assess your phone answering skills

▶ The skills required to answer the phone effectively and professionally

Preparing to Answer the Telephone

Proper telephone etiquette is a must and is crucial to the image of your company. Much of a company's communication is done over the phone: in the office, at your desk, in the car, at home, on a plane, and in this day and age, anywhere and any time. Effective phone skills can make or break customer relationships.

Nobody likes rude or discourteous people on the phone. This includes receptionists, sales clerks, operators, customer service representatives, managers, and co-workers.

Now here are a few key questions: Are you better than others on the phone? Do you serve your customers or co-workers (including the internal customer) with effective, polite, caring service? Are you creating moments of misery, mediocrity, or magic for others? How would customers rate you?

Like it or not, they *are* rating you, and they are rating your company based on their experiences with you.

It Starts with Preparation

Proper phone etiquette begins with thorough preparation before you answer or make a call. Positive self-awareness and the positive self-direction described earlier begin the process so you are more apt to have an upbeat, pleasing demeanor on the phone. The first step in satisfying the customer has nothing to do with the customer—it's all about you and your attitude.

You also need to know your equipment and have all of your materials available. Make sure you know how to:

- ▶ Put people on hold
- ▶ Transfer calls
- ▶ Include multiple callers
- ▶ Use the speaker phone
- ▶ Use the headset
- ▶ Adjust the volume
- ▶ Set up and check voice mail

KNOWING YOUR EQUIPMENT

If you don't know your equipment, you risk upsetting a customer by committing these common errors. Check those that have happened to you.

- ❑ Transferring and losing a customer
- ❑ Not understanding how to transfer and apologizing for it
- ❑ Not knowing how to put someone on hold
- ❑ Putting someone on hold and not knowing how to get the person back
- ❑ Interrupting someone else's call
- ❑ Picking up a call that isn't yours
- ❑ Losing messages in voice mail
- ❑ Thinking someone was on hold, when he or she wasn't—and the person heard you say things that you didn't want him or her to hear

Preparation Tips

▶ Practice using your phone in advance. Don't practice on customers.

▶ Keep your work areas neat so your computer, telephone, receiver, and head set are easily accessible.

▶ Adjust your headset microphone so it's comfortable but picks up your voice clearly. Hold the microphone portion of a telephone receiver directly in front of your mouth, and about an inch away. When you hold the microphone, make sure your hand doesn't cover it.

▶ Don't eat at your workstation. It's unprofessional to speak while eating.

▶ If you use a desk phone, don't use your cell phone in your work area or have personal conversations, Twitters, or text messages going.

▶ Don't use the speaker phone unless another person needs to be on the call. It's less personable.

▶ Before you start a day, and after lunch or breaks, refocus to stay positive with positive self-awareness and positive self-direction.

▶ If you are becoming too stressed, take a short break. Take a few deep breaths or get up and stretch for a minute.

TELEPHONE ETIQUETTE INVENTORY I

1 = Very ineffective, 2 = Somewhat ineffective,
3 = Neither effective nor ineffective, 4 = Effective, 5 = Very effective

Use the scale above to rate your skills:

_____ 1. Phone preparation: knowing the features of your phone

_____ 2. Answering the phone properly

_____ 3. Putting callers on hold

_____ 4. Transferring calls

_____ 5. Listening to the customer

_____ 6. Asking questions

_____ 7. Handling multiple lines

_____ 8. Taking messages correctly

_____ 9. Dealing with complaints or difficult situations

_____ 10. Using voice mail effectively

_____ 11. Staying positive on the phone

_____ 12. Using the cell phone effectively

_____ 13. Managing voice mail positively

_____ 14. Screening calls

_____ 15. Making calls for other people

_____ 16. Speaking clearly on the phone

_____ 17. Being courteous and polite

CONTINUED

____ 18. Leaving messages for others

____ 19. Leaving messages from yourself

____ 20. Checking messages and returning calls

What are your strengths? List four or five of the above items:

1. _____

2. _____

3. _____

4. _____

5. _____

What do you need to improve? List two or three of the above items:

1. _____

2. _____

3. _____

"Your call is important to us. Please stay on the line
until your call is irrelevant to anyone."

Phone Answering Skills

Some professions and jobs have stereotypical ways of answering the phone. Have you ever heard answers on the phone like these?

▶ **Customer service departments** — "To serve you better, please listen to these 32 options that have changed."

▶ **Sales departments** — "Yo, this is Billy Bob."

▶ **Technical help desks** — Ring, ring, ring, ring, ring, ring….

▶ **Management personnel** — "I will be out of the office today, July first. [It's now July 15th.] Please leave a message."

The above examples happen too often. Let's explore and work with four critical phone courtesies to help you be more effective. These take only a few seconds, but they make a big impression:

▶ The initial greeting

▶ Announcing your company or department

▶ Identifying who you are

▶ Offering to be of service to the customer

As we go through this part of the book, we will make it "live action." In other words, we will define each step, give you an example, and then ask you to script how you will answer the phone more effectively in the future.

> *I don't answer the phone. I get the feeling whenever I do that there will be someone on the other end."*
>
> —**Fred Couples**

HOW YOU ANSWER THE PHONE NOW

1. What is your initial greeting?

_____

_____

2. How do you announce your company or department?

_____

_____

3. How do you identify yourself?

_____

_____

4. How do you offer to be of service?

_____

_____

The Initial Greeting

Moments of misery:

▶ "Hold on."

▶ "Customer Service Department."

Moments of mediocrity:

▶ "Hi."

▶ "Hello."

Moments of magic:

▶ "Good afternoon…"

▶ "Good morning…"

Answer the phone in three rings or fewer: *This is the ideal.*
Why? Because then your customer doesn't have to wait too long. Waiting time seems longer on the phone than in person. If you can't do this and you know the customer has heard many rings, apologize.

Announcing Your Company or Department

Moments of misery:

▶ No department or company mentioned

▶ Talk too fast so no one can understand you

▶ Use an abbreviation that newcomers won't recognize

Moments of mediocrity:

▶ "Account number please?"

▶ "How can I help you?"

Moments of magic:

▶ "Good afternoon, Wonderful Company…"

▶ "Good morning, Customer Service…"

Identifying Who You Are

Moments of misery:

▶ No mention of your name

▶ Pausing after the initial greeting, waiting for the customer to do or say something

▶ Rushing through your name so the customer can't register it

Moments of mediocrity:

▶ "Doug speaking."

▶ "Rick here."

Moments of magic:

▶ "Good afternoon, Wonderful Company, This is Sue…"

▶ "Good morning, Customer Service, I am Bill…"

Offering To Be of Service to the Customer

Moments of misery:

▶ No offer

▶ "Can you hold?"

Moments of mediocrity:

▶ "What can I do for you?"

▶ "I will be with you in a minute."

Moments of magic:

▶ "Good afternoon, Wonderful Company, This is Sue. Where may I direct your call?"

▶ "Good morning, Customer Service, I am Bill. How may I be of service today?" Or "How may I help you?"

HOW WILL YOU ANSWER THE PHONE NOW?

1. How will you give an initial greeting?

_____

_____

2. How will you announce your company or department?

_____

_____

3. How will you identify yourself?

_____

_____

4. How will you offer to help the customer?

_____

_____

Phone Situations

In this section, we'll cover several situations: answering calls for people who aren't available; managing your tone of voice; creating your voice mail message; addressing others on the phone; and using someone else's phone.

Answering Calls for People Who Are Unavailable

Some of us might need to answer calls for others occasionally; for some of us, that might be the bulk of our job. Do you use good phone answering skills, as we have described? When answering someone else's phone, never explain the reason for the person's absence. It's enough to simply say one of the following:

▶ "She's not in the office today."

▶ "He's not available at the moment."

▶ "She has stepped away for a moment."

After giving the caller that non-informative information, follow it up with alternatives, and then with options.

Alternatives:

▶ "Perhaps I can help you."

▶ "Is there someone else you would prefer to speak with?"

Options:

▶ "Would you like to leave a message on his voice mail?"

▶ "May I take a message and have him call you back?"

Managing Your Tone of Voice

Tone of voice matters on the phone. As with many things in life, how you do something is as important as what you do. Visualize a representative answering the phone by speaking the following words in a quiet, monotone voice:

"Good afternoon, Furniture Plus. This is Sally. How may I help you?"

Say it yourself that way—out loud. (Go ahead and try it.) Not too impressive, is it?

Now imagine the same words spoken in an upbeat, enthusiastic voice. Say it out loud that way, too. Much better, right? Which would you rather hear as a customer?

The quality of your voice tone is made up of:

▶ **Rate of speech** — People in western English-speaking countries typically speak at about 125 words a minute. That's regular speed for most people. If you talk too fast or too slow, it can be an irritant to customers. Be conversational, and tape yourself at times to see how you come across.

▶ **Energy** — Be interested, positive, and excited about what you are doing. Try to bring a lot of energy to what you do. However, be realistic and don't be so perky and bubbly that you sound as if you are acting.

▶ **Pitch** — You can use low, moderate, or high pitch. Use pitch to help reflect the circumstances. If you have the same pitch all the time, it comes across as a boring monotone. If you have low pitch, you could be difficult to hear. If you have high pitch, you can come across as whining or screechy. So vary your pitch. Your initial answering of the phone could be high pitch. While you ask and answer questions, you might be more moderate. When dealing with a specific problem or emotional situation, you might use a lower pitch.

In each case, be genuine and be sensitive to the needs of the customer.

VOICE PREPARATION

Check the traits that apply to you.

❏ Enthusiastic	❏ Monotone
❏ Positive	❏ Nasal sounding
❏ Upbeat	❏ Raspy
❏ Clear articulation	❏ Choppy sentences
❏ Varies in volume	❏ Too quiet
❏ Friendly	❏ Demanding
❏ Easily understood	❏ Too loud
❏ Genuine	

The traits in the first column are desirable. Those in the second column will hinder customer service and are areas in which you need to work to improve.

Strengths (list two or three):

1. _____

2. _____

3. _____

Areas to improve (list one or two):

1. _____

2. _____

Creating Your Voice Mail Message

Know your machine or service, and follow these guidelines:

▶ Include these core courtesies in your message. "Hello, this is Mary in Customer Service. Thank you for calling. I'm sorry I'm unavailable at the moment. Please leave a specific message and I promise to get back to you within four hours." Note that your outgoing message is similar to how you answer the phone, but it adds a promise of follow-up service. Too many people don't do this because they don't check their messages often enough.

▶ Check your messages regularly. Do this multiple times a day to stay current.

▶ Get back to people promptly. If you don't have a complete answer for a customer request, don't wait until you do to call with an update.

▶ Record your own message and rehearse it a couple of times before you do it live.

▶ Always keep your voice mail up to date. For example, if you will be out of the office, you need to say that and give the customer the option of speaking to someone else.

YOUR VOICE MAIL MESSAGE

Write your outgoing voice mail message below:

_____

_____

_____

_____

_____

_____

_____

Addressing Others on the Phone

It's helpful to use the caller's name if he or she gives it to you. Why? Because it's more friendly. There are seven ways to address a caller; in the following list, ways 3–6 include the person's last name:

1. Sir

2. Ma'am

3. Mr.

4. Miss

5. Ms.

6. Mrs.

7. First name only

Many women prefer "Ms." Using "Miss" and "Mrs." can also be acceptable. How do you know which one to use? If a woman uses it as part of her name, then use what the customer uses. If you are uncertain, use "Ms." Some women are uncomfortable being asked "Is it Miss or Mrs.?" because they regard questions about their marital status as personal questions that are not appropriate in a business conversation. This is the reason that "Ms." was invented.

For men, it's okay to say "Sir" or "Mr."

Use a person's first name if the person says you can, if you have developed a good relationship with the person, or if you think you know the person well enough.

Answering Someone Else's Phone

When you answer the phone for someone else, use these same courtesies. However, instead of mentioning the company or department, use the name of the person. For example: "Good Morning, Ms. Smith's office. This is Joe. How may I help you today?"

Part Summary

In this part, we discussed how to be prepared to deal with people on the phone and how to provide SuperSTAR Customer Service. We also outlined the four courtesies of answering the professionally.

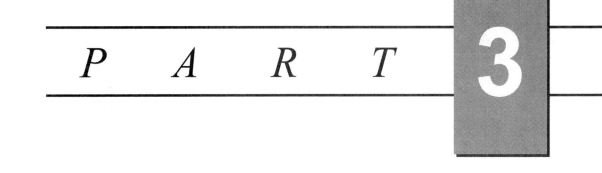

P A R T 3

Asking Questions and Listening Effectively

> *"There are no foolish questions, and no man becomes a fool until he has stopped asking questions."*
>
> –Charles Proteus Steinmetz

In this part:

▶ Why customers call and what they want when they do

▶ How to ask open- and closed-ended questions to get positive outcomes from your customer calls

▶ How to improve your listening skills

▶ Taking action based on your questioning of and listening to customers

What Customers Want When they Call

Your task on the phone is to help the customer. It's basic communication or a problem-solving process. Three skills affect face-to-face communication:

▶ **Words** — What you say affects 7% of your communication impact.

▶ **Tone of voice** — How you say your words affects 38% of your communication impact.

▶ **Body language** — What you do about what you say affects 55% of your communication impact. Body language poses a problem on the phone. You can't see the customers and they can't see you. So your words and tone of voice are even more important. However, by asking questions and listening effectively, you can overcome that barrier and demonstrate empathy and concern for customers.

What Do Customers Want?

Research by the University of Texas indicates that customers want five factors from service providers. We can remember these factors by the abbreviation RATER:

 Reliability. Do what you say you will do.

Assurance. Know your company, the products, the customer service policies, and the people.

 Tangibles. Make sure your equipment is working and your work space is neat and organized, so you are ready to help customers.

 Empathy. Provide care and concern for the customer's individual situation.

Responsiveness. Promptly answer calls, get back to the customer after a hold, and demonstrate a willingness to help.

RATER FACTORS FOR SUCCESS

Review the questions in the RATER factors below. Read the questions and answer each one so you can do a better job of helping customers on the phone.

Reliability:
Where can I improve in following through on my commitments? Personally? Professionally?

_____

_____

Assurance:
How can I improve my job knowledge? How can I improve my working relationships?

_____

_____

Tangibles:
What can I do to add value to my company by learning more about other areas? How can I improve my voice projection and quality?

_____

_____

Empathy:
What people skills can I improve? How can I be a better listener?

_____

_____

Responsiveness:
What can I do to deal with problems more effectively? How can I be of greater help to others?

_____

_____

Call Categories

Customer calls fall into one of eight categories:

- ▶ Information request

- ▶ Purchase

- ▶ Help that another person needs to provide

- ▶ Help with a problem that you can handle

- ▶ Complaint

- ▶ Asking for a specific person or department

- ▶ Misplaced call

- ▶ Other: _____

Many of these you can handle in a matter of seconds or minutes, depending on your job. Others take more time, and that's where your communication skills come in: asking questions and listening.

Ask Questions

Use questions to seek clarification or gain information from customers about their wants and needs. For example:

You: "Good Morning, ADS Group, this is Mary; how can I be of service?"

Customer: "I can't seem to make this thing work and the person at the store said it would."

You: [You don't really know what the person is talking about. You need to clarify.] "It sounds like you made a purchase at one of our stores recently. I am sorry you are having trouble. May I ask you a few questions so I can better help you?"

There are two kinds of questions: open-ended and closed-ended. Each can be helpful.

Open-Ended vs. Closed-Ended Questions

Use open-ended questions when you want customers to give you more information or explain what they want. Open-ended questions begin with:

▶ What

▶ Where

▶ Why

▶ When

▶ Who

▶ How

Use closed-ended questions when you need agreement on a specific fact or you want a yes or no. Closed-ended questions often begin with:

▶ Do

▶ Can

▶ Did

▶ Have

▶ Is

▶ Will/would

Good questions: *Get customers to talk about their needs. Build empathy as you listen. Understand and create trust as you work to help the customer.*

Let's review some examples:

Let's say the customer wants to check his bill. If you ask if he has his statement, the answer will be yes or no. Or you could ask "Can you give me the invoice number on your bill?" The answer will be yes (plus the invoice number) or no. These questions are closed-ended.

Another customer might need technical assistance with her computer. You might ask what she has done so far to try to fix the problem. "What is the error message that you receive?" These questions encourage the customer to explain or give more information. These questions are open-ended.

Both types of questions are useful on the phone. Use open-ended questions at the beginning of a conversation to better understand the customer's situation. Use closed-ended questions to pinpoint the issue or to gain agreement from the customer.

"Hi, you're through to Karen. How may I frustrate you today?"

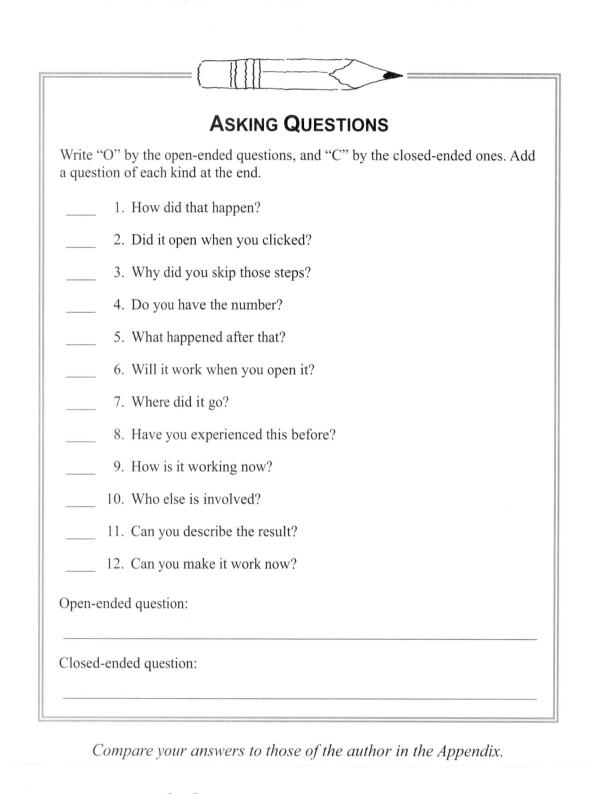

ASKING QUESTIONS

Write "O" by the open-ended questions, and "C" by the closed-ended ones. Add a question of each kind at the end.

_____ 1. How did that happen?

_____ 2. Did it open when you clicked?

_____ 3. Why did you skip those steps?

_____ 4. Do you have the number?

_____ 5. What happened after that?

_____ 6. Will it work when you open it?

_____ 7. Where did it go?

_____ 8. Have you experienced this before?

_____ 9. How is it working now?

_____ 10. Who else is involved?

_____ 11. Can you describe the result?

_____ 12. Can you make it work now?

Open-ended question:

_____

Closed-ended question:

_____

Compare your answers to those of the author in the Appendix.

**If The Phone Doesn't Ring, It's Me."**

–Song title by Jimmy Buffet

Listen

Listening has been called the master skill and the highest form of courtesy. It is important in person, and even more crucial on the phone. You can't see the person you are talking to, and a lack of listening communicates volumes about your desire to help. If you fail to listen effectively, the customer will feel:

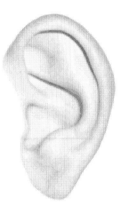

▶ Unimportant

▶ Irritated

▶ Upset

▶ Inclined to take their concern or business elsewhere

Your ability to listen will allow you to:

▶ Better understand the customer and how to help.

▶ Build better rapport with customers.

▶ Resolve problems faster.

▶ Answer questions more effectively.

▶ Feel more confident in your ability to communicate.

Listening is hard work; it takes practice to get better. Unfortunately, many companies tend to favor speaking skills more, although research says that 82% of individual people value good listeners over good speakers. In some firms, the definition of communication is two people talking at one another.

CASE STUDY: Listening Matters

One manager attended a seminar. The participants worked on listening skills by role-playing. The manager's role-playing partner began to cry. When asked why, she replied, "You are the first person to really listen to me."

Another manager did an internship for his Ph.D. in psychology by counseling AIDS patients. He told his friend that it was the most exhausting work he had ever done. The patients just needed someone to really listen to them and their life concerns. The more he paid attention and listened, the more it emotionally drained him.

Companies that succeed at keeping customers try multiple approaches—from focus groups to market research to online surveys—to listen to their customers. Many companies work to help their employees become good at listening to customers in one-on-one situations.

Many distractions can make good listening habits difficult, but not impossible, to maintain. What are some of the distractions?

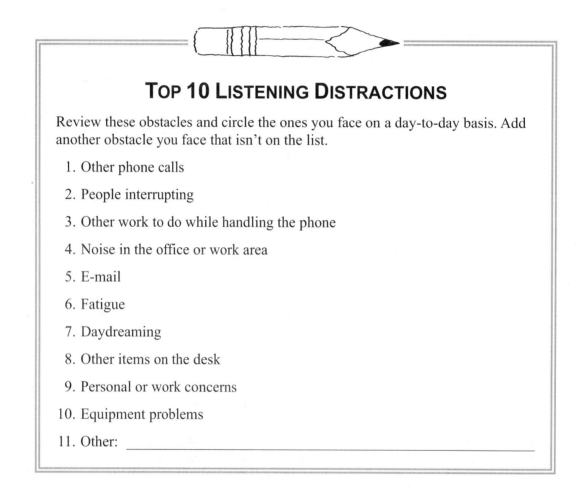

TOP 10 LISTENING DISTRACTIONS

Review these obstacles and circle the ones you face on a day-to-day basis. Add another obstacle you face that isn't on the list.

1. Other phone calls

2. People interrupting

3. Other work to do while handling the phone

4. Noise in the office or work area

5. E-mail

6. Fatigue

7. Daydreaming

8. Other items on the desk

9. Personal or work concerns

10. Equipment problems

11. Other: _____

To overcome these distractions, we will review the skills involved in listening.

Active Listening

To be an active listener, first organize your work space so everything you need is in front of you and easily accessible. Active listening means giving your undivided attention to the speaker to better understand the person's point of view. It helps to take notes, too. Jot down key points or names that your customer tells you, so you can better remember them.

Active listening also requires a few other skills:

▶ Good posture helps you pay attention.

▶ Use verbal cues to give feedback: "I see," "Okay," "I understand," "Tell me more," and so on.

▶ Ask questions.

▶ Empathize by acknowledging an emotional state: "I know this is upsetting to you."

▶ Paraphrase to demonstrate understanding: "What I hear you saying is…."

When the customer speaks, it will be easy for you to decide whether or not you are customer-centered. While you are on the phone, the customer is not right there in front of you. This makes distractions particularly hard to avoid and overcome.

Listening skills can keep you in the game so you can hit a home run for your customer. Check your listening skills in this exercise.

LISTENING CHECKLIST

Rate yourself on how well you listen. Answer yes or no to each question. Be honest and rate yourself on how you think you are, not what you think you should be. Use this exercise as a self-development tool.

	Y	N
1. Do you want to listen?	❑	❑
2. Do you put what you are doing not just aside, but out of sight?	❑	❑
3. Do you ignore or eliminate distractions?	❑	❑
4. Do you use nonverbal cues?	❑	❑

CONTINUED

	Y	N
5. Do you ask questions for clarity or to get more information?	❏	❏
6. Do you let other people finish what they are saying?	❏	❏
7. Do you restate or paraphrase what the person is saying?	❏	❏
8. Do you withhold judgment about the person or the problem until the person is finished speaking?	❏	❏
9. Do you listen regardless of the speaker's accent or tone?	❏	❏
10. Do you listen whether you agree or disagree with the speaker?	❏	❏
11. Do you ask what is meant by some words or phrases to minimize misunderstandings?	❏	❏
12. Do you listen even when you anticipate what the person will say?	❏	❏

List three or four strengths you have as a listener:

1. _____

2. _____

3. _____

4. _____

List two or three areas in which you can improve as a listener:

1. _____

2. _____

3. _____

CASE STUDY: A SuperSTAR Telephone Contact

Customer:	Dials company A.
Tech Support:	"Good Morning. Company A Tech Support. This is Rick, how can I be of service?"
Customer:	"I just ordered your software but it didn't download. I can't find it."
Tech Support:	"I am sorry about that, sir. May I ask a couple of questions?"
Customer:	"Sure."
Tech Support:	"First, when did you order the product?"
Customer:	"Just a few minutes ago."
Tech support:	"What happened when you downloaded it?"
Customer:	"I received package B but I couldn't find A. It seemed like it downloaded because it took 15 minutes."
Tech support:	"You should have received an e-mail confirmation with an order number on it. May I have your name and the order number?"
Customer:	"My name is George Jones and the number is AX8RUD1."
Tech Support:	"Thank you Mr. Jones. Now if I understand you and the information I see in my log, you ordered the DEX2 package about an hour ago, and began the download process. You received package B, but A didn't come through, correct?"
Customer:	"That's right, I got the one but not the other."
Tech Support:	"What I can do is send you the order with the download link and your activation codes so you can do it again. Does that sound okay?"
Customer:	"Great, I just want to make sure it works."
Tech Support:	"Okay, here it comes now. You should have it in a few seconds. Are you comfortable that this will help, or do you want me to stay on the line?"
Customer:	"No, I can handle it now."
Tech Support:	"My name again is Rick at extension 242 if you need further help. Is there anything else I can help you with? Thanks so much for your business Mr. Jones. Have a great day."

In this case study, what did Rick do well? He used the four key courtesies to answering the phone. He paid attention to the customer's problem. He was a good listener and paraphrased the problem. He offered a solution and gave his name for follow-up if needed. He asked if the person needed any other help and thanked the customer for his business. Wow!

To listen, you must want to listen. Your goal is to genuinely help the person you are talking to. All superstar customer service reps are extremely good listeners. Listening is not about agreement; it's about understanding.

One additional tip: When you listen, use the person's name. Doing so demonstrates a positive connection and interest.

Now, do you really care enough to pay attention through good listening?

Take Action

Someone once said that the great end of life is not knowledge but action. After you have answered a call professionally, listened effectively, and asked questions for understanding, you need to act. Help the customer. This could mean:

▶ Simply transferring the call immediately after your greeting

▶ Asking questions and listening to the customer's concern, and transferring the call to an appropriate person to handle this situation

▶ Taking the time to help the customer yourself, and doing whatever it takes

In the previous case study, the Tech Support person recommended a course of action and gained agreement from the customer. In some cases, you might need to do some problem solving. This includes asking more questions to gain all the facts or to clarify the problem, listening more, and then deciding on a course of action. If you can, give the customer options. Customers like choices and feel more in control when they have them. This makes customers more satisfied about the help they received.

When you finish questioning a customer, recommend a solution, but let the customer choose. Summarize to gain agreement. Find out if you can help with anything else, and thank the customer sincerely for his business or for calling. Always let the customer hang up first.

Putting the Caller on Hold

You might need to put a caller on hold to get more information, to ask for help, or to handle another call. If so, follow these steps:

1. Ask the customer if you can put her on hold for a minute (not a moment).

2. Wait for a reply—don't just automatically do it.

3. If the customer can't hold or doesn't want to, try to handle the situation, or take her name and number so someone else can call her.

4. Tell the customer she will be on hold for a minute. If it's longer than that, get back on the line and give an update.

5. When you get back on line, thank the customer for holding, apologize, and give an update.

Actions to Avoid

Bad habits that you might not even be aware of might offend a customer. Avoid the following at all costs:

▶ Eating or drinking while on the phone

▶ Letting your phone ring and ring and ring

▶ Becoming too buddy-buddy with the customer

▶ Speaking too softly

▶ Using slang or offensive language

▶ Telling jokes

▶ Talking to someone else while on the phone

▶ Putting the customer on hold by placing the receiver on the desk

▶ Speaking too loudly

▶ Telling the customer your problems

▶ Criticizing others in your company, or criticizing other companies

▶ Allowing too much background noise, such as a radio

▶ Using e-mail, text messaging, or Twitter while working with the customer

Treat the customer with the platinum rule: Give much better than what's expected. If you make a mistake, admit it, or if someone else made the mistake, apologize anyway—you work for the same company. Then make a commitment to fix it.

> *People used what they called a telephone because they hated being close together and they were scared of being alone."*
>
> **–Chuck Palahniuk**

Making a Call Back

Sometimes you can't do everything you need to do to take care of the customer in one call because you have to do research or talk to others to get a resolution. In that case, part of taking action is deciding on a follow-up plan with the customer. To do so, follow these steps:

1. Use the customer's name and explain that you will need to call back after doing some research.

   "Ms. Cane, now that you have described what you want, I know it will take some time to get this done. I will need to review the files and talk to the quality department. Then I can call you back with the specifics."

2. Ask if it's okay to call back after you do your research.

   "I apologize that I can't do it all now, but I can get more options by doing the research. Will it be okay for me to call you back?"

3. Set a specific time that's convenient for the customer

   "What is a good time for you tomorrow? How about 1:00 p.m? Great! I appreciate your flexibility."

4. Follow up. Organize your time, and schedule the call. Send a follow-up e-mail message if appropriate.

Part Summary

In this part, you discussed the RATER factors, which are keys to what customers want. You also reviewed important skills for asking questions and listening to meet customers' needs. You then learned about the key actions that satisfy customers and the actions to avoid. Finally, you learned about the importance of following up.

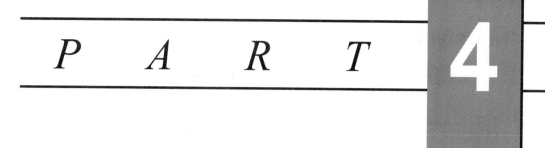

Handling Customer Moments of Truth

> *There is only one boss. The customer. And he can fire everybody in the company from the chairman on down, simply by spending his money somewhere else.*"
>
> –Sam Walton

In this part:

▶ Assessing your own customer focus

▶ The seven moments of truth for customer service on the telephone:

    ▷ Transferring calls

    ▷ Taking messages

    ▷ Initiating customer calls

    ▷ Handling problems

    ▷ Returning a customer call

    ▷ Using e-mail to support your phone contacts

    ▷ Upgrading cell phone etiquette

Customer Focus

So far, we have reviewed and practiced key basics of being a superstar on the phone:

▶ **Keeping a positive attitude** — Effective customer service begins with a positive first impression with an upbeat, enthusiastic outlook about yourself, the customer, and your job.

▶ **Answering the phone brilliantly** — Through four key courtesies, you answer the phone clearly and effectively to engage the customer every time, every day.

▶ **Asking questions and listening effectively** — These skills are intertwined and are crucial to building customer rapport and exceeding customers' expectations.

In this part, you'll learn about the seven moments of truth in relation to telephone customer service. But before we get into these, let's do a quick exercise to ensure that we keep a customer-focused approach all the time.

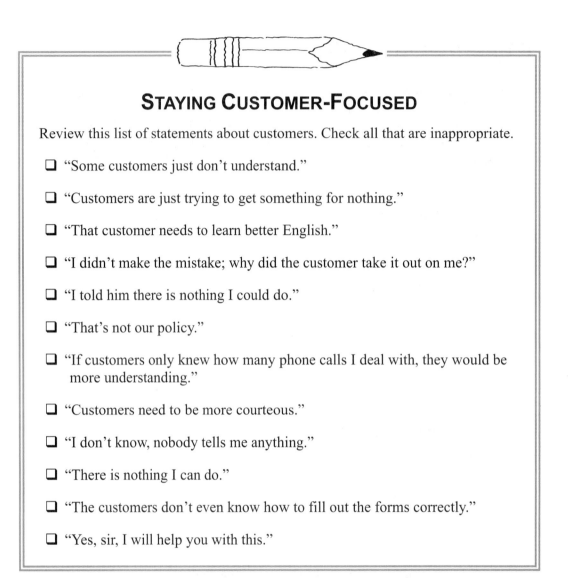

STAYING CUSTOMER-FOCUSED

Review this list of statements about customers. Check all that are inappropriate.

❑ "Some customers just don't understand."

❑ "Customers are just trying to get something for nothing."

❑ "That customer needs to learn better English."

❑ "I didn't make the mistake; why did the customer take it out on me?"

❑ "I told him there is nothing I could do."

❑ "That's not our policy."

❑ "If customers only knew how many phone calls I deal with, they would be more understanding."

❑ "Customers need to be more courteous."

❑ "I don't know, nobody tells me anything."

❑ "There is nothing I can do."

❑ "The customers don't even know how to fill out the forms correctly."

❑ "Yes, sir, I will help you with this."

Compare your answers to those of the author in the Appendix.

Moments of Truth

You will make a fantastic impression by being positive, answering well, listening, and using questions effectively. This impression will set you apart from others. But you are not done yet. The next set of skills involves all of the other daily activities you do on the phone to satisfy and keep customers. These skills include:

1 **Transferring calls**

2 **Taking messages**

3 **Initiating customer calls**

4 **Handling problems**

5 **Returning a customer call**

6 **Using e-mail to support your phone contacts**

7 **Upgrading cell phone etiquette**

Transferring Calls

Good communication is the key to transferring calls. Transferring calls gets the customers to the right person to help them as quickly as possible. Customers don't want to be passed on endlessly and wind up with someone who can't help them.

Too many people transfer without warning. Here is a poor example, or a moment of misery. This begins after a call has already been answered:

> **Customer:** "May I speak to Jill?"
>
> **Customer service:** "Hold on." The transfer is made.

This is rude and discourteous. There is a much better way to make sure the customer feels valued and well taken care of. Follow these guidelines:

1. Know your system, and know how to transfer calls. Most phone systems have unique and different options. So get help, study, and practice doing it right.

2. If you are in a position to help, ask. But include "Yes" in your answer. If you simply say, "Is there anything I can help you with?" some customers might interpret that to mean, "No, you can't speak to Jill." Instead, agree to the transfer, and follow up with an offer of help, almost as an afterthought: "Yes, I can transfer you. Oh—is there anything I can help you with?"

3. If you can't help with the customer's problem at this point, ask the name of the caller, use it, and ask if he or she can hold while you transfer the call. "Who is calling please? Mr. Johnson, can you hold while I transfer you?"

4. Put the person on hold.

5. Transfer the call.

Announcing a Call

In some situations, the people you transfer call to, want you announce the call before you make the transfer. Executives or managers often require this. You still transfer the call, but you talk to the person before you do. Follow steps 1–4 above, dial the extension, and tell the person who is calling. If she accepts the call, transfer it. If not, return to the caller and say, "Thank you for holding. Ms. Elliot is unavailable at the moment. May I take a message or would you like her voice mail?"

Taking Messages

Taking messages is a lost art today because calls are often transferred to voice mail. Your job may require you to take messages regularly or only on occasion. Regardless, it is important to get accurate and complete information and to get it to the intended person as quickly as possible. Have you ever received an incomplete message, or missed a message entirely? How did you feel? How do you think the customer felt about you and your company?

APPROPRIATE AND INAPPROPRIATE MESSAGES

Which of the following messages are appropriate?

1. "Joe called."

2. "612-314-8888"

3. "Please call Brian, at 602-788-1234. Signed, Sue."

4. "Jim Miller/Alert Business, 702-9876-0003. Ext.123. He needs the Invoice report for August ASAP. Signed, Darrin/9:30 a.m. Sept.7th."

Compare your answers to those of the author in the Appendix.

What are the ingredients of an effective message? Most message-taking slips provide an outline for this material. If not, make sure you provide it anyway:

▶ First and last name of the caller

▶ Company or organization, if appropriate

▶ Area code and phone number, and extension if applicable

▶ Brief description of the need

▶ Date and time of call

▶ Sense of priority

▶ Best time to call back, if appropriate

▶ Your name, and contact info if needed

Initiating Customer Calls

Sometimes your job may require you to call the customer first. Reasons for initiating customer calls are listed in the following exercise.

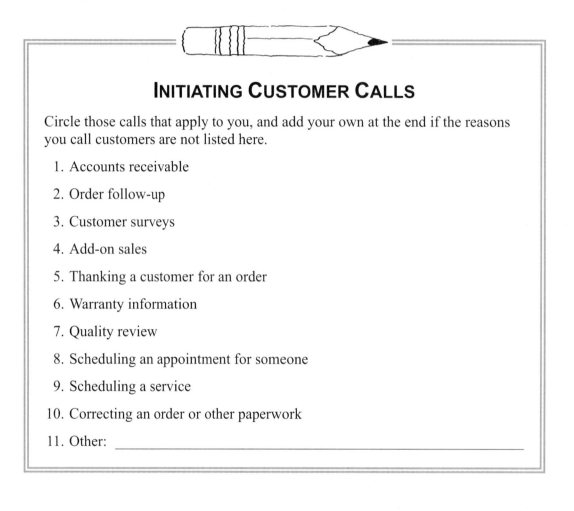

INITIATING CUSTOMER CALLS

Circle those calls that apply to you, and add your own at the end if the reasons you call customers are not listed here.

1. Accounts receivable

2. Order follow-up

3. Customer surveys

4. Add-on sales

5. Thanking a customer for an order

6. Warranty information

7. Quality review

8. Scheduling an appointment for someone

9. Scheduling a service

10. Correcting an order or other paperwork

11. Other: _____

Key Steps for Initiating a Customer Call

Making customer calls requires time management skills, especially if your job requires you to answer incoming calls as well. Calling a customer is a proactive process. When you receive customer calls, it's reactive; you don't control when a customer calls or how many customers call.

You need to schedule each outgoing call. This will keep them a priority. The best way to schedule calls is to block out, on your daily calendar, the times that are the best times to reach your customers or that will interfere least with incoming calls or other duties.

Then make sure you are prepared. Have your customer information available, either online or in a file folder.

Next, be clear about your goal. If you're calling the customer about changes in a product warranty, be prepared so you know all the details and know that they fit the kind of customer you are calling.

Here is a summary of the steps:

1. Greet the customer, using the customer's name.

2. Identify yourself and your company. Then take "the curse" off the call by asking if this is a good time or asking if the customer has a few minutes to talk.

3. State the reason for your call.

4. Take care of business.

5. Summarize or recheck agreements, if appropriate.

6. Make sure the customer has your contact information if needed.

7. Thank the customer for his time or business, and close the call.

Here's an example that puts it all together.

"Good morning, Mr. Rodriquez. This is Natalie Connor from AZT Stores. How are you today? …Great… Is this a good time to talk? I'm calling to ask a few questions about your recent visit, and this will only take a few minutes. My first question is…. Thank you for taking the time today, and I will pass on your comments about our customer service desk. If you need to reach me for any reason, my name again is… and my number is…. Have a nice day."

WRITING A CALL SCRIPT

If you make outbound customer calls, write a script for a call in the space below. Scripts are word-for-word outlines of your calls. Scripts can help you improve your efforts. Check your script with a co-worker or your boss.

_____

_____

_____

_____

_____

_____

_____

_____

_____

_____

_____

Leaving a Message for a Customer

Research finds that only one out of three business calls gets through to a live person. This means you will be leaving messages. Here are a few considerations:

▶ Identify yourself and your company.

▶ Speak normally, but slow it down a bit and strive to be clear.

▶ Leave your phone number. *Recite it slowly, as if the person listening to the message was trying to write it down!* Add the best time to reach you.

▶ State the reason for your call. Be brief and to the point.

▶ Focus on one thing you want the caller to do in response to the message.

▶ Leave the date and time you called.

▶ Be positive and make a good impression. Remind the person who you are.

Handling Problems

Inevitably you will come across problems when you talk to customers. Problems are more challenging on the phone because some customers are bolder on the phone since you can't see them. In two of our other books, *SuperSTAR Customer Service* and *Handling Difficult People and Situations*, we cover this issue in much more depth.

To begin with, try to stay calm. If the customer is upset and angry and you get that way, too, it will only make matters worse. So breathe slowly, remind yourself that it isn't personal, and remember how you would want to be treated if you were the customer: with care. Follow these two steps:

1. Deal with the person.

2. Deal with the problem.

There are two steps because when a customer complains, you always have two problems—the problem itself (what the person is calling about) and how it affects the customer personally.

Deal with the person

1. Listen. Use good listening skills, as we have discussed. Let the customer vent and get it out. Ask a few questions to clarify the issue. Paraphrase the issue and use the customer's name. Using a person's name makes the discussion more personal and can help people stay in control of their emotions.

2. Make a statement about feelings. This will help show empathy. "I know you are upset about this." "I understand that this is an inconvenience to you."

3. Apologize. "I am sorry this happened." "I apologize for the product being late."

Deal with the problem

1. Fact-find. If necessary, ask more questions to be sure you understand the issue. Ask the customer what he wants. Summarize your understanding.

2. Offer options to the customer. Give the customer a couple of ways to solve the problem. Recommend one of them.

3. Take action. Do something to move the issue forward. Decide how to help, or get a supervisor involved. Assure the customer that you will see this through, and then do so.

Returning a Customer Call

Return all calls within a minimum of 24 hours. (Of course, it would be best to return calls within the hour or at least on the same day.) One salesperson from IBM had this tagline on his voice mail message: "I promise you I will get back to you within four hours." This person was able to do this. That's superstar service!

Keep your voice mail message up to date. Don't have old dates or times on the message; it's unprofessional. Also, as you return calls, delete your messages. Have you ever called someone only to hear a voice mail system say, "This extension is full"? This is also unprofessional and sends the message that you are unable to take care of your customers.

"Alright, I promise not to imply that the tech solution is obvious."

Using E-mail to Support Your Phone Contacts

Most businesspeople have access to e-mail, either at home or at the office—often both. Worldwide, nearly 1.5 billion people use e-mail, and the number is growing. Nearly 50 billion e-mail messages are sent every day (not counting spam). E-mail far outstrips the postal mail in number of messages sent.

> *Have you ever wondered which hurts the most: saying something and wishing you had not, or saying nothing, and wishing you had?"*
>
> **–Unknown**

Use e-mail to support your phone contacts if it will add value. How do you know if it will? Here are several situations in which you can use e-mail to add value:

- ▶ You have information the customer needs.
- ▶ You need to update customers on your progress in helping them.
- ▶ You want to document (put in writing) statements, promises, or agreements.
- ▶ You want to thank customers for their business or feedback.

Notice that we didn't include "You want to get more information from the customer." Try calling first. Then send the e-mail message and mention that you called.

Structure the e-mail message properly. It should be similar, though not identical, to a business letter. Include the following:

- ▶ A specific subject line, such as "Inventory Report Deadline" or "Order Confirmation"
- ▶ A greeting
- ▶ An outline of what you want or need, in the body of the message
- ▶ Bullet lists for key points
- ▶ An appropriate closing
- ▶ A P.S.
- ▶ Any appropriate attachments needed

Sample E-mail Message

To: Dick Lewis@msp.com
From: Sue Weisman@xyz.com
Subject: Saturday's Meeting Agenda
Attached: Warranty Document

Hi Dick,

I hope all is well. I will call you for our discussion tomorrow at 1:00 p.m. I look forward to discussing your concerns in these areas:

1. Order accuracy
2. Warranty issues
3. Future orders

Attached is the new warranty document I mentioned. Let me know if you have any questions.

Sincerely,

Sue
XYZ Company
223-332-0101

P.S. I look forward to talking with you and appreciate your patience as I have researched your concerns.

Classic E-mail Caveats

- ▶ Humor depends on things like tone of voice and body language. These don't come across in a written message, so humor often doesn't work online. Don't risk it unless you are confident that the reader knows you very well.

- ▶ WRITING IN ALL CAPS IS THE EQUIVALENT OF SHOUTING!!!

- ▶ Your e-mail program probably includes a spelling-checker. Use it, even for short messages. Faylure to doo so can make yoo look unprofessssional, layzee, or baddly edyoocated.

- ▶ Accidental use of the "Reply All" function has been the source of more misery and embarrassment than all the celebrity gossip tabloids on earth.

- ▶ If you are angry or upset while writing an e-mail message, you might be sorry if you send it. You will hardly ever be sorry that you waited an hour or even a day to review and rethink what you wrote.

Upgrading Cell Phone Etiquette

The cell phone gives customers another way to contact a company representative. The advantages include:

- ▶ Direct access
- ▶ Faster access
- ▶ Shorter response time
- ▶ More personable approach

There is one problem, though. Cell phone users often take a more informal approach to answering their cell phones, so they skip appropriate phone etiquette. Proper phone techniques and etiquette are equally important on the cell phone.

TOP 10 CELL-PHONE ETIQUETTE MISTAKES

Circle those areas of cell phone etiquette that you need to improve; then commit to improving. Add one item of your own.

1. Talking too loudly or softly

2. Not turning off the ring tones in meetings

3. Answering the phone inappropriately

4. Talking about business or personal things in the wrong places

5. Letting the cell phone interrupt face-to-face conversations

6. Using ring tones that are inappropriate in a business setting

7. Talking while driving, and thereby becoming distracted

8. Having an unprofessional outgoing voice mail message

9. Not telling the people you're talking to that you are on a mobile phone so they are aware that there might be broken conversation

10. Not telling others that you need to take an important call

11. Other: _____

How did you do? What do you do well? How can you improve? The cell phone is a great tool; just follow the phone etiquette guidelines we have discussed, and you can be sure of making a positive impression on your customers.

Part Summary

In this part, you learned about seven moments of truth (including transferring calls, taking messages, and handling problems) and the strategies to turn them into moments of magic for your customers. You also worked on various exercises to improve your efforts in each of these areas.

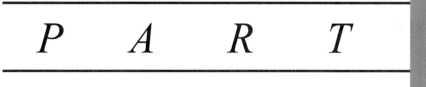

P A R T 5

Adding Value

> "If you're not serving the customer, your job is to be serving someone who is."

> —Jan Carlson

In this part:

▶ Skills you can use to communicate positively with others

▶ How showing customer appreciation adds value

▶ How to follow up and follow through, showing your customers that you are reliable

▶ Why going the extra mile matters

▶ What you can do to foster internal teamwork that will add value for your customers

Five Strategies for Adding Value

What separates you from others? Why would a customer want to work with you? In this book, we have defined moments of magic as ways for you to distinguish what you do on the telephone from others so you can help your company do the same. All of our efforts are intended to ensure customer loyalty and repeat business.

George Allen, famed former football coach of the Washington Redskins and Los Angeles Rams, was always good at taking a losing team of veterans and making them winners. He was asked how he did it. His reply: "We always did one more."

He meant that they worked harder at practice, studied game films, made plans, and prepared. People don't become superstars in customer service just by showing up. They become superstars by working hard, continuing their education, persisting in the face of obstacles, and focusing on their goals with resolute determination.

We will review five strategies to help you add value while you continue to improve. These powerful strategies are:

▶ Communicating positively with others

▶ Showing the customer appreciation

▶ Following up and following through

▶ Going the extra mile

▶ Creating internal teamwork

Communicate Positively with Others

A motivational speaker challenged his audience, "Is there anyone out there who can't get along with others? Please stand up." No one did. The speaker repeated the challenge, and waited, and finally one man in the back stood up. The speaker moved forward on the stage and asked, "Sir, you mean you can't get along with others?" The man replied, "Sure I can, but I felt sorry for you standing up there alone!"

Everyone thinks they can get along with others. Unfortunately, local and global events show otherwise. The world stage includes constant struggles and distant wars between and within nations. Local news media are too often the spotlight for highlighting crime, family turmoil, gang battles, school violence, and political bickering. Are people really getting along?

Research by Daniel Goleman in his books on emotional intelligence identifies the importance of social competence, or people skills, in career success. He defines this as empathy—the awareness of other peoples' feelings, needs, and concerns—as well as social skills and adeptness at inducing desirable responses in others.

Your ability to communicate with and get along with others does make a difference, doesn't it?

TELEPHONE PEOPLE SKILLS

1 = Very infrequently, 2 = Infrequently, 3 = Neutral, 4 = Frequently, 5 = Very frequently

Using the scale above, rate yourself on these people skills:

_____ 1. Listening to others

_____ 2. Understanding others' needs

_____ 3. Helping others based on their needs

_____ 4. Recognizing the positive contributions of others

_____ 5. Offering helpful feedback to others

_____ 6. Being willing to coach or mentor others

_____ 7. Providing excellent *internal* customer service

_____ 8. Providing excellent *external* customer service

_____ 9. Treating all people with respect, courtesy, and dignity

_____ 10. Valuing diversity in people

_____ 11. Challenging the biases and prejudices of others

_____ 12. Creating teamwork with others

List two or three of your strengths:

1. _____

2. _____

3. _____

List one or two areas in which you could improve:

1. _____

2. _____

Show the Customer Appreciation

Unfortunately, customers get a bad reputation at some companies, with some people. One manager we worked with called his customers "bananas." When asked what he meant, he said they always complain about anything. Not surprisingly, employees also called customers "bananas." After further investigation, we found that the customers definitely had reasons to complain, because the company wasn't good at customer service. We helped the company managers realize that they had to get better to reduce customer complaints. Customers weren't bananas. They just wanted better service.

We need to debunk three myths about customers:

▶ Customers try to make things difficult on purpose.

   Most customers are just trying to reach you, get want they want, and be treated respectfully and courteously.

▶ Customers like to complain.

   Research says that 96% of customers are silent complainers. In other words, they don't complain to the source, but they do tell their friends or family about their poor service experiences.

▶ Customers expect the impossible.

   We reviewed earlier what customers want. The impossible was not listed. They do want what they paid for. If you deliver that and do it with a little pizzazz or thoughtfulness, you will usually outshine most other service providers.

Showing customers appreciation demonstrates your commitment to improve and do a good job of thanking customers for their business.

Your Commitment to Continuous Improvement

Why does this matter? If you keep trying to give better service through phone skills, you will provide more value to the customer. The best way to think about this is to remind yourself how you want to be treated. How would you like any of the following moments of phone misery?

▶ Abrupt answering

▶ Getting cut off

▶ Rude behavior

▶ Being passed around on the phone to multiple people

▶ Voice mail messages that aren't returned

▶ Excuses for lack of action

▶ Being put on hold abruptly or for too long

▶ No apologies for problems

▶ Lack of follow-through on promises

What have you learned or relearned about handling the telephone? In the following exercise, review and identify the concepts you will continue to work on. Do this with joy and not as a chore. Your company depends on you, and your career success depends on your personal accountability and responsibility to raise the bar of your effectiveness and performance.

" *Treat every customer as if they sign your paycheck, because they do.*"

–Anonymous

WHAT I HAVE LEARNED OR RELEARNED

Review parts of the book and write three or four specific things you learned in each part. For example, in the Introduction, we presented the definition of SuperSTAR customer service as, "The goal is to treat customers much better than they expect by self-managing five Moments Of Magic."

Introduction:

_____

_____

_____

_____

Keeping a Positive Attitude:

_____

_____

_____

_____

Answering the Telephone Brilliantly:

_____

_____

_____

_____

CONTINUED

===== CONTINUED =====

Asking Questions and Listening Effectively:

_____
_____
_____
_____
_____

Managing Customer Moments of Truth:

_____
_____
_____
_____
_____

"I'm Judy and I'll be your pain in the neck for the next five minutes."

Ending a Phone Conversation: Thanking the Customer

One of the most important parts of ending a phone conversation is thanking the customer. It seems basic and simple, but it's powerful. Why? Next time you're the customer, observe how many times people thank you for your business. Too often, it's the customer thanking the business for its help.

We want customers to feel good about the phone contact in two ways:

▶ How you treated them

▶ What you did to help them

How do you thank customers? Do it sincerely and do it often. Say it on the phone and send e-mail to express your appreciation as well. Here are some examples:

▶ "It's been a pleasure serving you. Thank you for calling."

▶ "Thank you so much for calling STP Company."

▶ "Mrs. Customer, we appreciate your business. Thanks for calling. Have a nice day."

▶ "Goodbye for now. You and your business are appreciated."

▶ "Thanks for your time and business today. Please call again any time."

CASE STUDY: Cowtown

One company that we'll call "Cowtown" wanted to make sure that employees thanked customers. So they held a meeting and told every employee to remember to say, "Thank you for shopping at Cowtown."

Management threatened to fire employees who didn't comply. The employees didn't like that approach, and one employee made a card that showed only the initials of the phrase: TYFSAC. This employee then pronounced these letters to customers instead of saying the actual words. Of course, customers who heard this walked away confused. Before you knew it, employees in every location were doing this to customers. Its effect on customers was quite the opposite of what management had hoped.

(The real name of the company was left out to protect its identity.)

Thank customers genuinely, and they will notice. It will have a positive effect on them. Do it because it's the right thing to do and not because you have to. Also vary how you say it, depending on the situation. If you don't, you will become a little robotic. Remember, a positive, upbeat, honest thank-you always adds value.

Follow Up and Follow Through

One of the key service issues for customers is reliability. In others words, do what you say you are going to do. In service, you must keep commitments. You must follow up and follow through. If you don't, it affects your credibility and integrity and your company's.

We have discussed some crucial telephone follow-up techniques: callbacks, making sure someone follows through on a message, getting back to people on hold, and returning calls to customers. So let's do an activity to generate other methods you can use.

RELIABILITY: FOLLOWING UP AND THROUGH

Check the methods you can use. Do all of these apply? What else can you do?

_____ 1. Say thank you in a variety of ways.

_____ 2. Send a follow-up e-mail message with a thank you.

_____ 3. Give the customer a compliment.

_____ 4. Ask the customer if there is anything else you can do to help him.

_____ 5. After a few days, call the customer back and see if everything is okay.

_____ 6. Solicit help from a co-worker and ask that person to call the customer.

_____ 7. Make sure the message you left for a co-worker from a customer is followed up on.

_____ 8. Call a customer and provide an update on your progress to help her.

_____ 9. Recommend a solution to the customer.

_____ 10. Tell the customer how he can save money with you on promotions he might not know about.

_____ 11. Other: _____

_____ 12. Other: _____

Go the Extra Mile

Going the extra mile means performing above and beyond the call of duty. This is also how to exceed a customer's expectation and keep customers.

GOING THE EXTRA MILE

What can you do? Ask your supervisor and get a clear picture of how far you can go to keep a customer. Find out how "empowered" you are. Write those expectations in the space provided.

_____

_____

_____

_____

_____

_____

_____

_____

_____

_____

Real Examples

Here are some real examples of going the extra mile in various industries:

▶ **Airlines** — When delays occur, the counter attendant can give out perk coupons.

▶ **Car dealership** — The salesman delivers the car to the customer's home and puts on the license plates.

▶ **Restaurant** — The restaurant gives away a free dessert for a customer's birthday.

▶ **Supermarket** — If a customer leaves an item at the checkout, have it delivered to their home.

▶ **Hotel** — Make free, freshly baked cookies available in the evening.

▶ **Credit card company** — Waive a service fee for loyal customers.

▶ **Yard maintenance** — Provide literature about products that would help the homeowner's yard.

▶ **Electronics store** — Hold free seminars that describe new technology.

▶ **Pet store** — Give dog biscuits to dogs that customers bring into the store.

▶ **Clothing store** — Provide comfortable chairs so that customers can rest.

▶ **Bank** — Hold customer appreciation days with special loan promotions, finance seminars, and information packets.

Wow the Customer with Kindness!

The customer is king. Just ask any businesses having a tougher time or closing their doors because of financial woes. Did you know that the greatest challenge facing companies engaged in customer service improvement is complacency? Being good is the greatest enemy of excellence.

A book called *Random Acts of Kindness* captured the attention of many when it was published. The author suggested that we go out of our way to be helpful or kind to others without being rewarded or even known. The book was written to counteract the random acts of violence seen in too many places. The author suggested that if we do this, we create a better world.

Superstar service involves *planned* acts of kindness. Conduct yourself with the noblest of purposes to be kind and friendly. It's the right thing to do. If that's how you consistently do things, you will become legendary—known for going the extra mile.

> *If you don't care, your customer never will."*
>
> —**Marlene Blaszczyk**

Create Internal Teamwork

You get teamwork by giving it. You need teamwork to serve the customer better on the phone. Without teamwork, your job becomes lonely and isolated. It's no excuse to say that others don't do it. It begins and ends with you. First you reap, and then you sow. How do you get started?

1. Learn the names and jobs of as many people as you can. Ask others to introduce you. Seek out new people in meetings. Call and introduce yourself to people you send calls to. This helps you when you transfer calls or take messages.

2. Attend all training sessions that are related to your job so you learn about other areas of your company.

3. Make a commitment to deliver moments of magic to all internal customers. Treat them all with the utmost respect, courtesy, and dignity.

4. Ask others how you can serve them better. Learn their likes and dislikes in terms of what you do for them. This information will help you understand how to communicate with them about customers you have talked to or helped.

INTERNAL CUSTOMER PERCEPTIONS OF ME

Answer the following questions as honestly as possible.

1. What is it like to be served by you as an internal customer?

_____

_____

_____

_____

2. How would others rate you?

_____

_____

Become a Team Player

Everyone seems to agree that teamwork matters. Unfortunately, 70% of organized team efforts in companies fail. There are common traits that can guide you. Why is this important and even worth mentioning in a book about telephone skills?

First, if you help others, they are more likely to help you. It's what the platinum rule is all about. Go out of your way to serve others with exemplary style, and when you need help, others will want to assist you because of how you treated them. You will be able to take care of your customers better and will become known as reliable and dependable.

Second, when you transfer calls, be sure that others take care of those calls. When you leave messages and assure the customer that a problem will be handled, your reputation is at stake, too. When you need support to learn how to help a customer, your internal network will come to your rescue. This doesn't happen overnight. Go through a relationship-building process with the people you work with. If others experience you as a superstar service provider time and again, not only will they return the favor to you, but you will also set an example for them to follow.

Teamwork

A group of people working collaboratively toward common goals.

TOP 10 TRAITS OF TEAM PLAYERS

Put a plus sign by the traits you think you have. Put a checkmark by the ones you need to develop. Take heart; no one is perfect. Anyone can become a team player with hard work and learning. Teamwork is about commitment, not perfection.

_____ 1. Trustworthy

_____ 2. Caring

_____ 3. Open and willing to share

_____ 4. Dependable and reliable

_____ 5. A student of your field, with technical competence

_____ 6. Hardworking

_____ 7. Positive and upbeat

_____ 8. Good at communication

_____ 9. Receptive to feedback—good or bad

_____ 10. Participating and involved

List two or three of these traits that you see as your strengths.

1. _____

2. _____

3. _____

List one or two areas in which you need to improve.

1. _____

2. _____

Multiply Your Efforts with Telephone Teamwork

The truth is, you are in business for yourself even if you work for someone else. You aren't doing it for free; you need to make a living. You are your own corporation. Incorporate yourself! While each individual must accept personal accountability and responsibility for his or her job and life, the help of others is also important.

It's been said that two heads are better than one, and a triple-braided cord is not easily broken. You can succeed alone, but you'll multiply your success through the help of others. The key word is network, network, and network. Do this both inside and outside your company. In other words, make a consistent and persistent effort to make new friends and meet other people. At work, meet as many people as you can in the company. In sales, for example, the most successful salespeople get referrals. This means that loyal customers give them the names of other people who could use their products or services. You will build more customer loyalty in your job with great teamwork inside the company.

Before you begin or expand your efforts to personally market yourself, consider this philosophy. Motivator and author Bob Conklin built two nice-sized companies from scratch and wrote numerous articles and books. His business philosophy stated, "Help other people become successful, and you'll be successful." First you give, and then you get. Teamwork is an unselfish process. The goal is to help your customers, co-workers, friends, and colleagues to achieve their goals. In return, they will be more willing and happy to assist you. Let's get started doing the exercise on personal marketing for teamwork.

PERSONAL NETWORKING FOR TEAMWORK

Identify 15 people you know whom you can help, and identify how you can help them. Then, identify how they could help you. Remember, give unselfishly, and then, at the appropriate time, ask for assistance or support. In the spaces below, list the people's names, ways you can help them, and ways they can help you. Now, get started; take action!

Name	How to help	Assistance to you
1.		
2.		
3.		
4.		
5.		
6.		
7.		
8.		
9		
10.		
11.		
12.		
13.		
14.		
15.		

Part Summary

In this part, you learned about and worked on five strategies to add value. Anybody can help a customer once. A SuperSTAR goes above and beyond. By applying these added-value approaches to your customers, you will gain more loyalty and business from them.

A P P E N D I X

Appendix to Part 2

Assess Your Progress!

In Part 2, you took this inventory of your telephone skills. Take it again and observe your progress and achievement.

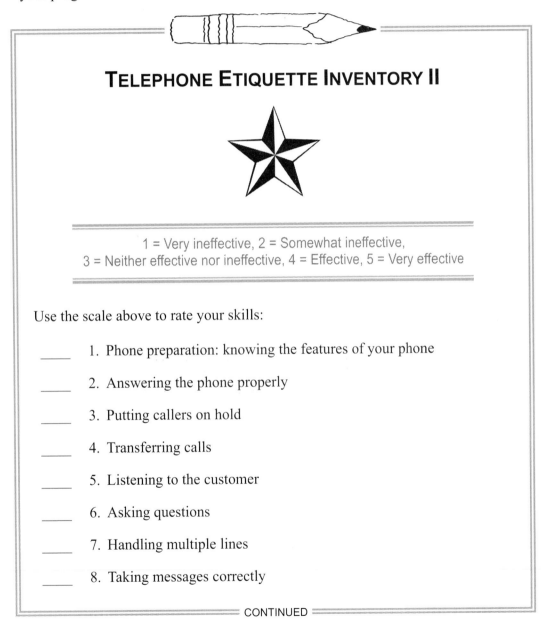

TELEPHONE ETIQUETTE INVENTORY II

1 = Very ineffective, 2 = Somewhat ineffective,
3 = Neither effective nor ineffective, 4 = Effective, 5 = Very effective

Use the scale above to rate your skills:

_____ 1. Phone preparation: knowing the features of your phone

_____ 2. Answering the phone properly

_____ 3. Putting callers on hold

_____ 4. Transferring calls

_____ 5. Listening to the customer

_____ 6. Asking questions

_____ 7. Handling multiple lines

_____ 8. Taking messages correctly

CONTINUED

CONTINUED

_____ 9. Dealing with complaints or difficult situations

_____ 10. Using voice mail effectively

_____ 11. Staying positive on the phone

_____ 12. Using the cell phone effectively

_____ 13. Managing voice mail positively

_____ 14. Screening calls

_____ 15. Making calls for other people

_____ 16. Speaking clearly on the phone

_____ 17. Being courteous and polite

_____ 18. Leaving messages for others

_____ 19. Leaving messages from yourself

_____ 20. Checking messages and returning calls

> *Do what you do so well that they will want to see it again and bring their friends.*"

—Walt Disney

Appendix to Part 3

Comments & Suggested Responses

Asking Questions

The author categorizes the odd-numbered questions as open-ended, and the even-numbered questions as closed-ended.

Appendix to Part 4

Comments & Suggested Responses

Staying Customer-Focused

The only truly customer-focused statement is the last one. The rest are excuses from employees with poor attitudes. The last statement ("Yes, sir, I will help you with this") clearly demonstrates the approach of customer service superstars. Regardless of difficulties, they go out of their way to positively and cheerfully help customers.

Appropriate and Inappropriate Messages

The first three messages are poor examples—more moments of misery. Too much information is missing. Message #4 is the best of these.

Appendix to Part 5

Apply Your Telephone Skills

Satisfy your customers and keep them coming back! SuperSTAR Service is a choice. After deciding that you want to be as good as you can be, you have worked through this book and done the exercises. That's commitment. Nice job!

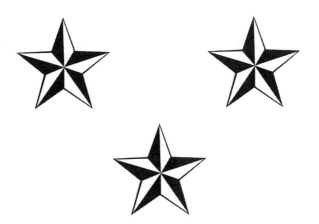

Obviously it doesn't end here. Every day there are phone calls to receive and phone calls to make. Every day there are customers to serve and co-workers to team up with. That's, of course, if your company continues to get better in helping customers. You play a huge role in that, as we have discussed.

We have covered five crucial aspects of providing customer service through the use of the desk telephone or cell phone.

1 **Keeping a positive attitude!** You control your attitude, regardless of the circumstances. It's a choice. Through positive self-awareness and self-direction, you can stay upbeat and optimistic. By focusing on your goals, strengths, and successes, you become stronger and more self-assured. The first step in taking care of the customer has nothing to do with the customer; it has everything to do with you.

2 **Answering the telephone brilliantly!** How the phone is answered is often the customer's first impression of your company. Like it or not, the bottom line for you is that the level of service you provide affects the success of your company and your career. There are four key courtesies in answering the phone; use them.

3 **Asking questions and listening effectively!** Your communication with customers involves asking questions and listening. Use open-ended and closed-ended questions to understand the customer better. Listen by paying attention, taking notes, and paraphrasing to make sure you know what is wanted and needed.

4 **Handling customer moments of truth!** We discussed and practiced seven moments of truth related to using the phone: transferring calls, taking messages, initiating calls, handling problems, returning calls, using e-mail as support, and maintaining cell phone etiquette. All of these might take only a few minutes of time individually, but they are best practices that will help you help customers.

5 **Adding value!** It's been said that we must under-promise and over-deliver. The new adage is "over-promise and over-deliver." This is all about giving added value. In this part, we reviewed key communication skills, showing customer appreciation, following up and following through, going the extra mile, and creating internal teamwork. These five strategies will help you wow your customers.

Make a Plan for Success!

Finally, make a plan to succeed. The implementation and use of new ideas or skills is what matters most. We can know what to do, but if we don't do it, there is little value to be gained. It's been said that persistence and determination are omnipotent. Create a SuperSTAR Telephone Plan, and may the best of success be yours!

SuperSTAR Telephone
Action Plan for Success

Describe the actions you will take to apply SuperSTAR Customer Service to using the phone in your job. Then, review your plan with your supervisor and co-workers. Finally, act—deliver moments of magic to your customers.

1. What I've learned or relearned (review Part 5):

   _____

   _____

2. Identify how you'll implement each of the five strategies with customers (be as specific as possible):

   a. Keeping a positive attitude: _____

   _____

   b. Answering the telephone brilliantly: _____

   _____

   c. Asking questions and listening effectively: _____

   _____

   d. Handling customer moments of truth: _____

   _____

   e. Adding value: _____

   _____

Additional Reading

Crisp 50-Minute Series books:

Rick Conlow and Doug Watsabaugh. *SuperSTAR Customer Service*.

Rick Conlow and Doug Watsabaugh. *Handling Difficult People and Situations*.